Badger

ENCOUNTERS IN THE WILD

JIM CRUMLEY

ONE

MIDWINTER BADGER SETTS HAVE A comatose air. The badgers themselves are often inclined to hunker down on a night like this one, what with sleety squalls and a foul-mouthed wind barging gusts through the big trees, tugging the clouds apart into sudden scraps of moonlight.

That on-off moon was over my shoulder and the wind mostly in my face, so in the unlikely event of a badger shrugging off the warm torpor of the underworld for a rumble around the sodden overworld I inhabit, I was in a good place.

I had taken precautions enough to last for perhaps three hours – a good insulated mat to sit on, enough layers of clothing to impress a polar bear, a flask of coffee, a second flask of something twelve years old and Hebridean, and shortbread fingers by the handful for emergencies.

This was a spur-of-the-moment enterprise after a chance encounter with an acquaintance who thought that badgers in this neck of the Trossachs woods were struggling a bit, and did I know why? I didn't, I said; didn't know they were struggling and didn't know why, if they were. I could ask a few people or... or I could take the temperature of a favourite sett in a woodland clearing with a helpful mound in one corner, where I could sit facing a west wind and a few feet below the top of the mound so that my shape didn't break the skyline.

I don't use hides for watching badgers, don't climb trees, don't perch on dykes or cliffs or up stepladders (I know badger fanatics who insist on one or all of these). I like being part of their land-scape, which means not hiding from them, not trying to be something other. But it also means establishing a low-profile presence, so stillness, silence and a capacity to do nothing at all but watch and listen and think for a few cooling hours are the pre-requisite tools.

BADGER

I had used moonlight to install myself, walking in along the fence at the bottom edge of the clearing. I got comfortable – a relative term in the circumstances – and put a notebook, pencil and wee torch in my lap, just in case something turned up and I wanted to write it down. So now I was ready to grow cold, slowly.

Time was suddenly elsewhere. The night lost all its points of reference. There were black walls of trees, there was a marginally less black sky, there was the voice of the wind, and there was that moon's struggles to hold its own against hurtling masses of cloud. The clearing was reduced to vague undulations that generally sloped uphill and away from me, its duvet of bracken flattened and tea-stained. The sett's entrances were in the crown of the clearing about seventy yards away. I could see nothing else at all. So I sat and waited for something to turn up.

I love this part of the job.

I love the fact that I have a job that allows me to sit and do nothing for hours at a time, as many of them as I can thole, and there is nothing and no one haranguing me to get back to work, to do something useful, to make something worthwhile out of my shift. This *is* me working. This is me reverting to type, donning ancestral garb; this is me becoming Nature, subsiding down through all the intervening sedimentary layers of society's accumulated detritus that we have built up to defend ourselves against the fearful prospect that, one day, we might be compelled by circumstances beyond our control to become Nature again. In the event that such circumstances arise during my lifetime, I should be better prepared than most.

The first obvious symptom of the process was physical. I started to see with night eyes. The shroud of trees that hemmed in the clearing on three sides began to resolve into individuals: I could tell the pines from the larches from the oaks from the beeches. Suddenly there was a rowan tree twenty yards away that I had not noticed, and not remembered from previous visits.

Then I started to hear better. The wind was now many voices rather than just one loud, gusty blare. There were higher pitches among the canopies, deeper and throatier booms among trunks and limbs, a rustle of rowan spindles, a thin whine by my upturned collar. This is how it works.

Then there was a barn owl on a fencepost. My first "something" had turned up, although I didn't see it arrive. It was on the furthest post, a yard inside the corner of the clearing. It must have swerved low around the last tree while the moon was in "off" mode. For a handful of seconds, its soft-white face and breast were moonlit and, not for the first time in my life, I thought that perhaps it was the most beguiling creature in all the wild-wood. Then a new blast of the west wind sounded, the moon guttered out and the owl was grey, and without the knowledge imparted by that moonlit glimpse, it could have been anything at all.

Clouds thickened and settled lower. The wood blackened a little, the clearing dulled down, and night clenched its fists and took a tighter grip on the place. A new squall scudded round the edge of the wood and dived into the clearing with relish, firing buckshot into my face. For a while, the only sound was the bouncing hiss of sleet-bloated rain.

ENCOUNTERS IN THE WILD

◉ ◉ ◉

The wind was quietening, one consequence of which seemed to be that the squalls had abated and evolved into steady rainfall. I looked for the owl but it was gone. I did not see it go, any more than I saw it arrive. I consoled myself with coffee, a mouthful of whisky, then an ill-judged mouthful of shortbread that did not go down quite as nature intended, and induced a spasm of coughing. In my efforts to muffle the sound I spilled coffee over my notebook and waterproof trousers and I swore a lot under my breath, and, just possibly, over it.

It was all too much noise and too much move-ment, revealing much too much of my presence on the mound. At that moment, at the very nadir of the evening, even as I wiped my trousers, stowed the flasks and the notebook and shoved the rest of the shortbread in my mouth (taking more care with the crumbs this time), something shifted at the top of the sett. I sensed it rather than saw it, but once I focussed my binoculars, there were three badger heads in an entrance, each head immobile, each pair of badger eyes staring in my direction.

BADGER

There is a surreal quality about the first emergence of a badger on a midwinter-dark night, a quality that is quite absent among the broad-daylight badgers of spring and summer. The first thing you see is two or three disembodied patches of white, and whether two or three depends on whether the badger is side-on or head-on. Head-on is best because then the patches form a kind of mask shape, widely spaced at the top (separated by the two broad, black face stripes) and tapering towards the bottom where all three finally meet just above what will prove to be the badger's snout. But this white mask is still underground, for the emerging badger pauses just inside the sett entrance for several seconds or several minutes while it evaluates the scents of the night. When it does finally emerge, what follows the well-defined mask is a bulky, dark-grey, shapeless blur. Only if your night-sight is fully attuned is the often surprising size of the creature apparent.

Generally, they materialise slowly and gently. And then – slowly and gently – you become aware that you are smiling to yourself, for a newly

emerged badger is the most smile-inducing creature I know.

So now, my one hope lay in the knowledge that
they could not smell me, and that badger eyesight
is not the most acute of their senses. What they
might make of my shape in the darkness need
not necessarily mean that they recognised me for
what I am. They had certainly heard me, but all
they heard was a cough, a syllable of muttered
Anglo-Saxon and a certain amount of indetermi-
nate rustling.

They loitered just inside the entrance, waiting
for reassurance. Then, one by one, they emerged
onto a badger-fashioned terrace in front of the
entrance, one by one they shook themselves in the
rain, one by one they started to walk westwards
along the terrace, and one by one they disappeared
back underground via the very next hole.

I gave it another hour. A field mouse came by
and scoffed what I think must have been some
shortbread crumbs, probably a career first for the
mouse. A roe deer barked out in the field and drew
an answer from somewhere far behind me.

BADGER

Enough. I packed up and headed out to the steep woodland path that led down to the distant road and my car. Four hours, more or less to the minute.

The engine muttered into life, my headlights blazed into a line of trees, and I had no more idea than I did when I started whether or not badgers were struggling in this neck of the woods, and if so, why. I knew there were at least three. I knew that two years before there were at least twenty. And I knew a little more about the nature of night in such a midwinter woodland, a little more about nature in the woods on such a night, a little more about how far your species and mine must travel to reclaim our oldest inheritance. I considered all that a reasonable return for the night's work.

TWO

I CAME LATE TO BADGERS. I had been deterred by a grotesque experience when I was about fifteen. I had found a derelict cottage when I was out on a bike ride. There was an old water butt in what had been the garden. I peered inside. It was full of water in which there floated the bloated, maggot-seething corpse of a badger. I had never seen anything quite so grim. Then a robin flew down, perched on the corpse, deftly filled its beak with maggots and vanished. By the time it was shoving them down the throats of its brood, I was being sick in the nettles. It seems strange to me now that it should put me off badgers rather than robins.

Thirty-something years later, I wrote a book called *Waters of the Wild Swan* (Jonathan Cape, 1992), which consummated my passion for these wondrous birds. I had been greatly assisted in that project by a man called Brian Cadzow, who

farmed at Glendevon in West Lothian. A pair of
swans that nested on the old millpond outside his
window had provided one of two focal points of
my early swan-watching years. From time to time
during our many conversations over fist-sized
whiskies he would ask me:

"Have you ever written about badgers? No?
You should. Super creatures."

I resisted the idea politely, several times, but
Brian persisted several times plus one. Then he
showed me four setts, and with no effort on my
part I was handed a passport into the world of
badgers at the sett. But I was curiously unmoved
by this generous gesture that handed me badgers
on a plate: I convinced myself that I needed to
find my *own* way into that world. So I began again
with landscapes of my own choosing. The first
was among fields and low hills cut by slow waters
and well-hedged lanes, where a dark, holly-strewn
wedge of unkempt land I called the Holly Glen
seemed to form a natural centrepiece. I had eyed
it speculatively already and found badger tracks,
an old hole that could have been an outlier of a

sett, and enough hints of badger visits to reward closer scrutiny.

And I decided (for no good reason) that if I thought of the Holly Glen as a kind of fulcrum of the local landscape, it was reasonable to believe that it was also central to the badger's idea of the same landscape. Watching badgers at the sett – like watching birds at the nest – is one thing, but what really appealed to me was to encounter the badger out on his rounds, the freewheeler of the woods, the fields, the open hillsides, to see him with his fellow travellers, to watch him at work.

There were three badger-fashioned paths in the Holly Glen, one up each side and one right through the central mass of holly, a bottle-green tunnel. They all met at the top of the glen's small hill and entered and left the glen as one. From there, that deeper-worn path abruptly turned at right angles under a fence and headed west by a field edge. This became known in my personal geography of the place as the Crossing. And there, on the bottom strand of fence wire was a small knot of snagged badger hairs. I removed these carefully and leaned three twigs against the wire, like a set of miniature wickets on the path. If it was a regular badger route, they would barge the twigs aside and more hairs would snag on the fence. Next day the sticks were down, and the next. As often as I replaced them after that, they were down again within a day or two, and from time to time there was a new badger hair caught on the fence wire. It was time to stake out the Crossing and learn.

But when to watch? The times badgers emerge from their setts, the reasons for those times, the changing patterns of those times from season to season, and the inexplicable lapses in those patterns, are the stuff of expert and inexpert theories. Badger-watching, I soon discovered, is awash with both species of theorists. So the first thing I learned was to turn deaf ears and shut up. I wanted to write a book about finding out about badgers. I reasoned that I was dealing with a tribe of individualists with individual habits, and in nature the whims and wiles of individualists make mockeries of received wisdom and expert theories. I invented my own, of course, but

ENCOUNTERS IN THE WILD

I discarded them as fast as I invented them, and slowly I replaced them all with a growing admiration for the elusive object of my good intentions. The problem of when to watch was compounded by not knowing where the sett was. Nor did I know when the badgers emerged from it, nor how long it took before they left its vicinity to forage, nor how long it might take them to travel for however far it might be. Finally, I discovered that what worked best was being lucky.

Mid-March midnight was blue-black and cold. Stubble crackled under my feet. I made too much noise as I walked. I slowed my pace, placed my feet more carefully. The last of the land before it tipped into the Forth lay in intimate folds. I sat for the fourth consecutive badgerless night by the Crossing. I had begun watching from six o'clock till nine, then seven till ten, eight till eleven, and now I was working the nine till midnight shift. I sat above the Crossing on a small bank, the wind pushing my scent away east – apparently confident the badger would approach downwind. I can no longer remember why I thought that.

BADGER

Ground mist was a problem so close to the firth at that time of year. It was difficult to focus on mist when there were no focal points. I tried to imagine where the extended line of the path beyond the Crossing burrowed into the nearest patch of mist, and focussed there. The close call of an owl, or a field mouse rustling behind my back, were apt to jerk my head round at first, but eventually I succumbed to the demand for utter stillness and began to resist such things.

In that prime spell of the watching, every sense strained for messages and night-sight grew more efficient. Finally, I saw a badger shambling to the field edge. His swaying walk shouldered a furrow through the mist that closed at once behind him, and his double-striped white face nodded at each stride like a Clydesdale. He walked head down, but he paused often to listen and test the breeze.

Ten feet away from the Crossing, and just when it seemed he must trundle straight to the fence and squirm under it, scattering my sticks, he suddenly bounded left, shot through the hedge (a gap unknown to me until that moment) and into the bottom field with a startling turn of speed.

I sat another cold hour, wondering what had betrayed me. Whatever it was, it was enough to convey an implied threat to the badger. Sight is the sense he relies on least and he would have wanted a scent or a sound from my shadowed shape on the bank. He got what he wanted and bolted for cover, perhaps to a burn-side hole I had found in the bottom field, where he would have had to knock over two more of my sticks. I imagined him there, deep in the dark earth, facing the entrance, holding his curiosity in check, waiting until he urged himself on again, up and out of that safe darkness into the wide open fields. Perhaps he would have made for the Holly Glen by way of a scramble up the burn bank and under the fence, catching another neck hair on the bottom wire and leaving it there for me to find in the morning. I duly found it.

I waited yet another hour. Lapwings moaned in the high field where they stood through the darkness of the high-tide hours, lifting stiffly in small, slow squadrons to glide a dozen yards to a new stance. That final hour grew uncomfortably cold and I abandoned it when uncontrollable shivering ended any serious prospects of staying still enough to do the job.

Trudging up the steepest of the field's switch-backs, weighing up the evening's events, I saw what may have been the same badger, just as it swayed in on the restlessly dozing lapwing flock. One bird lifted a few feet into the air then swooped to within inches of the badger's indifferent head.

I saw its pale breast dart down, shadowed by its own wings, saw the bird briefly mask the pale badger head as it danced close, saw the wings haul it clear again back to the flock, saw the badger head thrust on, low to the ground, nodding its perpetual affirmative. A lapwing about your head, it said, is nothing more than confirmation of supe-riority over lapwings. The badger had a more pressing concern.

I had turned further out into the field to detour away from the lapwing flock, but I had unwittingly ensured that my path would cross the badger's. Now his nose was to the scent of my diversion. It would tell him that I had passed very recently, that I was moving too slowly to have travelled far. This was a reasonable guess on my part: if I, a badger-watching novice, could tell from a set of badger tracks whether it was sitting, standing, scrambling, loping or running, how much more fluent must the badger be with the tracks of man, and with the one scent that he has so much cause to fear? So in his mind I was nearby and a threat.

He stopped, sat back on his haunches and listened, peering through a web of shadows, one of which was mine. I was close by the trees again, having rounded the lapwings, and I stood twenty yards uphill from him. He stared straight at me for a handful of seconds, then his eyes drifted on. Another lapwing reared up from the grounded flock, high enough for me to see its crested silhouette and dangling legs against the sky. It fell at the badger's head, so close that a turn and a snap would surely have killed it. But the badger's head simply watched and listened and scented among the shadows, and the lapwing was just one more flickering shadow.

BADGER

The movement forward of a sitting badger from hunkers to all fours is one of the most bear-like gestures he makes. Watching him at that moment, small in the open widths of field and firth and sky and night, I thrilled to a badger for the first time. I felt an eager edge about my quest. In that single gesture my work was handed the impetus it needed. The badger put his nose to my trail and came on, bear-bold, weasel-curious. Three times in those twenty meandering yards the badger sat and listened and tasted the air with his nose. Three times he stood, bear-like, and came on. He was six feet away when he stopped for a fourth time and detected the meaning behind my shadow. He gave a soft grunt, turned in his own length and *walked* away back down the field.

Not ran, but walked!

I stood as rooted as the holly at my back, while his bear-gait and broad beam dwindled methodically down the field. Once he stopped and looked back, half turned, and I willed him back, but he turned again and took to the very edge of the field where I lost him in shadows and mist.

Years later, long after my badger-watching had gravitated northwards to the Highland Edge and my constant presence on the territory of a particular group of badgers had established me as a benevolent element in their landscape, a big boar badger found me standing by a tree beside his preferred path in a very different field, and instead of avoiding me he simply peed on my wellies so that my smell was more acceptable to him. I chose to believe that I had been anointed. It was a long journey in so many ways, but it began that night of the low mist, the lapwings, and a badger that put his nose to my trail and came on.

THREE

THE BRACKEN HAD YET TO TURN. There was more than a lingering hint of summer to a warm early-September evening. The flies were as thick about my head as blossom on a May hawthorn. The surrounding spruces of a bleak forestry plantation contrived their own particular shade of gloom. The sun was already low and no shred or thread of it penetrated that crowding press of trees. The air had an uneasy, stifling feel I did not much care for, especially after three midge-stricken, badger-watching hours that had been utterly free of badgers. I was done. I had just decided that I was going for a cold beer on the way home. It was the first cheery thought of the night.

The way out was not a particularly pleasant prospect, for it lay along a forest ride where the bracken stopped but the grasses were waist-high and a wet ditch ran up the middle. In the dimming, greying half-light it was not that easy to see where the grass ended and the ditch began. It would be easy to succumb to an ill-considered mood of failure, but that is unworthy of the task in hand. Besides, moving carefully between walls of trees and wearing the same spruce-like shades, there is always the outside chance of catching something unawares, and if the wind is in your favour, so much the better. So don't switch off, not until you are far beyond the wood and back on the road to the car. It does not do to relax just because it feels as if the "official" part of the watch is over. The fact that I did not see a badger go or hear one stir does not necessarily mean that no badger went or stirred.

So I was still alert enough to hear the grass rustle and mutter, still alive enough to the situation to recognise that something other than the wind was at work. I froze. I rested my eyes on the spot without trying to make too much sense of it at once. In such a gloom, the eyes like to find their own definition of things, their own way of discerning truth from deception. The grass continued to move then it went quite still. By the time it moved again every blade was in sharp focus, and these slowly started to fall aside to accommodate a dark grey shape that paled and hardened into a badger head. A badger face was staring at me.

I have seen many variations on the theme of that face in many different circumstances. It is a face I have never learned to take for granted. Nor have I learned to be anything other than impressed by its bearishness, particularly when it masks the broad head of such a heavyweight boar. The half-light had the effect of magnifying him further and of brightening the white mask so that it looked briefly as if it was disembodied and existed separately from the dark bulk of the head.

Then he sat back. Just like that.

He did not run or panic or hide. He looked straight at me and he sat back. It was as if he had already sensed my presence, but given my dark shape and my slow and quiet passage through the evening, and with the light wind working against him, he advanced and sat, to see if his eyes could make anything out of my presence. There is also the possibility that because of my repeated forays around his territory over a couple of years he was accustomed to my scent and it no longer troubled him because all I did was walk quietly and sit still.

So he sat and I stood and we faced each other across the beginning of the forest ride, and somewhere between us a trickle of water muttered in the bottom of the unseen ditch. His sitting had a second purpose. When he saw me first, or rather when I first saw him looking at me (which may not necessarily be the same thing), he was side-on to me and his profile was low to the ground. Then, just before he sat he turned towards me, so that when he did sit back on his haunches his whole body was massed and curved behind his head, and being a heftily muscled beast, he suddenly looked three times the size of his side-on, low-slung self. The sitting was a pose designed to impress. It worked. He impressed me. Again.

He stared for ten, perhaps twenty seconds. He looked suddenly sideways, then back towards me. The grass moved again. The sow emerged. She padded over to him, parting the grass as she walked, leaving a padded-down track the width of herself behind her. She went and stood behind him and half-hidden by his bulk, she peered round his shoulder at me, her head lower and smaller and narrower than his, and the two masks might have been the grimaces of ghosts. Then she turned and trotted to the forest edge and stepped inside the trees. He lingered a few seconds, still staring, grunted quietly, turned away and followed her.

I knew by now they had two cubs, and I wondered how close these might be, and whether they too were in the grass and might respond to a summons from their parents. But there was no summons and the grass had stopped moving.

In the lull that followed a pair of woodcock hurtled up the ride and passed low overhead, matching wingbeat for wingbeat and coughing and squeaking, a curiously frog-voiced vocabulary for such elegant birds. With their passing, the forest seemed to acquire a new and muffling layer of night. The quiet deepened. I held still, trusting to instinct. I had done the hard work, I was in a good position; there were badgers around, so wait a little longer.

ENCOUNTERS IN THE WILD

The cracking of a twig focussed my attention back on the edge of the trees. They had not gone far. They might return. Then I wondered if I might lure them back. Biologically speaking, they are big weasels after all, and one thing a weasel cannot resist is something that rouses its curiosity. So I began to click my tongue and pop a finger against the inside of my mouth and whistle softly... anything that might fall curiously on listening ears. I could hear them inside the trees. They were not leaving, but were they coming back? I kept clicking and popping and whistling, and they shifted around inside the trees, but they stayed inside the trees too. Then, just when I thought I was getting nowhere, the woodcocks returned and their voices meshed with my percussive nonsense, and the boar's face was suddenly back, peering up from almost ground level beneath the lowest sweep of the spruce branches. Almost at once the sow was right beside him. Then came the cubs.

For perhaps ten seconds, no more, all four faces gleamed garishly out of the forest at me, and it was all I could do to stifle a laugh, for they looked like nothing so much as characters in a puppet theatre, and an absurd image came into my head of the puppet-master crouched behind them dangling two puppet masks on strings from each hand.

I have seen badgers and badger setts everywhere from high on a Knoydart mountainside to a mountain woodland in Balquhidder to the coast of Fife to Berwickshire, but nothing has charmed me so utterly as those ten seconds at the bottom of a spruce tree at the edge of the Trossachs.

The circumstances had as much to do with it as anything. I have already shared my disquiet at staking out a sett or a bird's nest, or in some kind of artifical set-up that persuades wildlife to linger. What delights me is this, this kind of chance encounter that sheds light on how the creature behaves out on its rounds, patrolling its territory, going about its business. I find my own instincts best served when I can just go and become, as far as is humanly possible, a discreet fragment of the natural world, a part of the landscape, because it is my chosen landscape too. My purpose, and therefore my reward, is to encounter wildlife on these terms – on the wildlife's terms – for in such circumstances that part of me which is still "nature" comes to the fore and briefly dominates mind, eye, sensibility, and – however briefly – dignifies the human breast.

The four badger masks withdrew, going backwards, and a curtain of night fell where they had been. I heard them shuffle away, heading back down through the trees towards the clearing where the sett lay shrouded in bracken. I listened until there was no more to hear.

SPELL FOR SAFE BADGERS

Roof well timbered
with root of limber tree.
Thatch of bracken.

Courage, stealth, health of cubs.
Wealth of places to dig and scratch.
Home patch lardered with worms.
Peace. Fleece of stars.

BADGER

Wind far-carrying. Cool marrying
of water and dark earth.
Dearth of gun, gas, dog, trap, poison,
noisome men and their sour scents.

Otherwise,
just leave us
alone.

FOUR

THERE IS a scruffy little country lane where I walk from time to time, knowing that I'm safe from all forms of wheeled transport other than tractors, and their reverberating growl is audible half a mile away so I hear them coming. At one point the lane dives into a tousie, dark wood, almost as if it is ashamed of its own scruffiness, as well it might be, but it has always had one saving grace. And now I know it has two.

The one I knew about before is that the wood accommodates a badger sett. Many of its forty or fifty entrances are very close to the wood's road-side fence, and here and there the badgers have dug under the fence and come up in the roadside verge. I have never seen them use the roadside holes, although it's clear from scrapings and rear-ranged fence wires on the other side of the road that they do cross to forage in that uncolonised half of the wood, and in the rough field beyond.

So I was walking the lane for no good reason except that I had been working nearby and found myself with time to kill and it was a morning that held the smell and the aura of a new spring. I wouldn't be seeing adult badgers at midday in April, but it had been a while since I was here and I thought I might check for signs of activity anyway. Besides, April is the cub month hereabouts; I could always look for the patter of little footprints. If you're lucky, you can stumble across unwary cubs at almost any time of the day, and when it comes to badgers, my track record has been a lucky one.

A well-honed sixth sense is among the most priceless of assets to a nature-watcher. The honing is the fruit of years, of patience, of ritual, of reworking a particular set of circumstances again and again and again, so that if something changes you sense it as readily as you might see or hear or touch or smell it or taste it on the wind. I was walking towards the wood, thinking about badger cubs, when it occurred to me that almost all the cubs I had ever seen have been in daylight and well away from the core of the sett. So instead of going into the wood I went looking for the entrances to the under-the-fence tunnels on the roadside verge.

Two I remembered were overgrown and unused. But there were also two I had not remembered, and these looked freshly dug, and there at the edge of the second one were some very small footprints indeed. Too small for badger. Besides, whatever the size of the badger, from venerable boar to weeks-old cub, a badger footprint looks like a badger footprint, and these did not. They belonged to what I now know to be the wood's second saving grace. I thought: "These look like..." and the thought remained unfinished because the face of their owner appeared in the mouth of the tunnel, saw me, and vanished.

I crossed the narrow lane away from the hole, stepped over the waist-high fence on the far side, stood next to a tree and waited. I waited because I had good reason to believe that the face would be back. I glanced at my watch, wondering how long it might take. I guessed: three minutes maximum.

It took a minute and a half. I saw some white fur first, then made out the two blackest eyes in the wildwood. These advanced none-too-cautiously into the daylight.

I whistled, clicked my tongue and made kissing noises. The creature advanced a yard out into the lane, stopped, stood on its hind legs and stared. Pound for pound, or in this case ounce for ounce, is there anything more fearless on earth than a weasel?

Its coat shone in a dapple of sunlight. It was sleek and skinny and it moved in wavelet ripples. It stood again and showed its teeth. But mostly it stared its black unblinking stare. I thought of it then as the most dynamic of all our native mammals, the most packed with purpose and energy, the blithest and most effortless athlete, the most confident in its own skin, the most un-deferential beast on four legs this side of… this side of… this side of nothing at all really.

It is also the nosiest creature in the wildwood, which is both part of its charm and, from time to time, the source of its downfall. For if I was keeper with a gun, or whatever it is a keeper uses these days to reduce weasels to corpses to hang on a barbed wire gibbet, that nosiness would have been a death sentence. As it was, I chatted away to the weasel and watched it come to within six feet of where I stood, sizing me up (its six inches nose to tail against my all-but-six-feet), obsessively determined to satisfy itself about the source of the noises and, if necessary, see it off. How much closer it might have come I don't know, but suddenly the ground began to shake and a tractor the size of a small farmhouse rounded the end of the wood and charged up the lane, towing a piece of outlandish machinery whose purpose quite baffled me. When it had been and gone there was just an empty lane, a drifting smell of diesel, and a thread of new footprints that disappeared deep into the hole.

I have heard of all kinds of creatures sharing a badger sett with the badgers, and seen some of them – fox, rabbit, once a hare during a storm, and once an otter – but I had not seen or heard of a weasel lodger. The late Ernest Neal[*], immortal world authority on badgers, had heard of it, but only on a very casual and temporary basis. His Europe-wide list of "mammalian tenants of setts" in his book *The Natural History of Badgers* (Christopher Helm, 1986) includes not just rabbit and fox, but wolf, porcupine, racoon dog, pine marten, polecat and wildcat. So the weasel is in tow with some fairly uncompromising company, especially when you add the badger itself into the equation. I was astounded to see badgers mentioned in the same breath as Siberian tigers in *The Great Soul of Siberia* by Sooyong Park (William Collins, 2016), when he was writing about the early lessons that the adult tigers teach new cubs, lessons which included "...that badgers are tasty but have a temper and a long sickle-like nail that can really cut you..." Thus the badger's reputation for fearlessness in a tight corner is ennobled in my eyes.

Mind you, the weasel's reputation is also built around punching above its weight. David Stephen*, who was a Scottish naturalist of distinction and a bit of a specialist in the weasel tribe, wrote of it

* *See Afterword for more on Ernest Neal and David Stephen*

thus in *The World Outside* (Gordon Wright, 1983): "…a mighty atom – a bantam sable, a mink in miniature, a 2–4oz mustelid delivering a thousand volts, a fire-cracker in brown topcoat and white waistcoat who can put the fear of death in many a grown man…"

John Buchan, who knew his way around the flora and fauna of the land, reached for the mighty atom to portray the mindset of his character Fish Benjie in *John Macnab* (Thomas Nelson, 1925): "…Benjie fought in no orthodox way, but like a weasel, using every weapon of tooth and claw, but in his sobbing furies he was unconquerable, and was soon left in peace."

I borrowed from the stillness of the tree where I leaned, I was tree-coloured in my clothing and although I dare say I did not smell like one, it seemed the stillness was enough, for in five minutes the weasel was back, lingered in the entrance for about ten seconds then advanced into the sunlight… followed at once by a single-file platoon of eight more weasels, which was presumably the whole family. They flowed along the lane in goose

formation, a rippling ground-level skein of tawny
and white, a breaking wave of terror in the collec-
tive awareness of the mice and vole population of
that place, and everything else up to and including
the rabbits, maybe even the hares.

Once I saw a weasel take on a rabbit, not fully-
grown but not small, and I would guess it was
a pound in weight to the weasel's two or three
ounces. You have doubtless heard of the weasel's
capacity to "hypnotise" a rabbit into stillness before
it strikes. This one used ambush as its preferred
technique. The rabbit was feeding on grass near
a stand of nettles. The weasel was hidden in the
nettles and charged from about a yard away, leapt
for the throat and hung on. The rabbit died slowly
and struggling violently, but the weasel hung on
and hung on. Then it contrived to drag the rabbit
into the nettles, and few things that I have seen
in nature have been quite so impressive, quite so
ruthless, quite so one-sided.

So, there is a scruffy little country lane I know,
and it has a dark wood with a badger sett, and
from time to time, the tenants from hell move in.

FIVE

RUMOUR had begun to harden into certainty, the way rumour does when it goes unchallenged. The badgers had gone from their long-established quarters in that clearing in a Trossachs wood, with which I began this account. The word that had reached my ears, admittedly third-hand, was that there had been a survey. The surveyor said there had been no badgers. The word got around.

There are two ways to respond to such news. You can trust the source and take it at face value. Or you can distrust the source. The survey found nothing and concluded that there was nothing to be found. I find fault with that methodology. Besides, I don't much care for wildlife surveys and I trust them less. They produce a snapshot of a moment in time in many different places. I work the opposite way. I produce many snap-shots in one place over many years, because I

believe the results are more trustworthy. It's why
I have chosen to work a territory for many years
now, crossing and re-crossing the same landscape, compiling and constantly revising a map
of what's where and how it interacts with everything else. The resultant knowledge is a kind of
intimacy. The only worthwhile way to conduct
nationwide surveys is for many people to visit
many landscapes many times, but they tend not
to have that kind of manpower, funding and the
necessary patience. Nor, for that matter, do they
have the necessary intimacy to reach the kind of
conclusions that anyone can trust.

So there had been a survey and it had concluded
that at the sett in question there were no badgers.
The conclusion surprised me. The sett is an old
one, and (at least until two years ago, when I was
last there) had been continuously occupied for
forty years that I knew of, and quite possibly for
several times forty years, for such is often the pedi-
gree of old and undisturbed setts. And this one is
undisturbed and well hidden and unless the estate
had taken a sudden dislike to badgers, it was not

immediately clear to me why they would leave. On the other hand, it does happen very occasionally that a sett will go "cold", but when it does, the explanation is – mostly – obvious and man-made. So I went in search of the explanation.

To reach the sett you enter an old woodland of oak and ash, beech and birch, sycamore and Scots pine, rowan and willow, and at once you must climb a steep bank about two hundred feet high. It was always well patched with wild hyacinths, which English mistakenly calls "blue-bells". But botanically they are wild hyacinths; bluebells are the ones that come out along coast paths and up mountains in high summer, though English mistakenly calls them "harebells". They have nothing to do with hares.

The evening was late April, sunlit, and blessed by an easy easterly breeze that suited my purpose. Even before I was in the midst of the trees, even before I reached that awkward little diagonal path with a mischievous runt of a rowan that fankles progress there, even before I had finished with the short stretch of narrow road between my parked car and the hidden way into the wood... even before any of that, I was drenched and dizzied by the strength of hyacinth scent. I could not remember encountering the phenomenon before, at least not here. But as soon as I entered the wood I realised why. The whole bank, top to bottom and edge to edge, something between a quarter and half a square mile, was a make-believe land of blue. I half expected hobbits.

Close up, the flowers were the deepest blue on earth, and so closely packed that to take any one step was to flatten a dozen and release fresh clouds of scent. But they paled into distance, and at the furthest reach of the wood the effect was of a swithering, lilac-shaded ground mist in which every tree trunk waded and every fallen trunk and broken-off limb was embalmed.

I sought out the beginning of a path the width of one walking badger, and which I know of old. From the top of the bank it descends at an odd angle, the first indication that it was not made by human passage as a direct route up and down the bank. Instead, it was designed to connect with a break in an old drystone wall, beyond which it squirms under a fence and emerges in an equally steep field of rough pasture. If the survey was right and there were no badgers in the sett, I guessed that the path would be swamped by the glacier of blue that had overwhelmed the bank, and that it would be difficult to find. But if its skinny diagonal was still clearly defined, that should mean that there were enough badgers nearby to have maintained one of their longest traditional routes.

Not all badgers from the same sett use all their paths all the time, and a sett like this one radiates paths to almost every compass point. Some badgers may never use some of the paths available to them. Some leave the sett by the same path every night. Even a single badgerless week at this time of year could be enough to dull the path's imprint, such was the fecund growth on the woodland floor. I looked back down the bank behind me and there was barely a hint of my passage as breeze-fashioned eddies drifted the flowers across my footsteps.

BADGER

Then a holly tree stood before me and I remembered that the badger path veered away just above it en route to the broken wall and the field. So I skirted round the tree and there was the path.

But its presence was inconclusive. The flowers had been parted, but there was not a scrap of bare earth, and what I had remembered was a path of bare earth. The effect was of a ghost path. So perhaps there had been a hiatus, or perhaps there were too few badgers to maintain a path so far from the sett, or perhaps they just avoided it when the flowers were in their prime because such a weight of hyacinth scent compromised their sense of smell, which is such a crucial element of their way of life. I know badger paths that trudge through patches of wild garlic and I imagine that is equally overpowering, but as soon as the patch is behind them the wind restores to them a virtuosic repertoire of scents. But the sheer scope of that growth of wild hyacinths might well have inhibited them from travelling there.

That was the frame of mind I brought with me as I descended the far side of the bank and closed in on the clearing that accommodated the sett. The clearing is gently domed and the heart of the sett was always under the shallow dome, where a single rowan tree offered a simple marker from a distance. As soon as I could see the tree I stopped, put my back to a sycamore trunk, and studied the clearing through binoculars. At that distance it did look un-lived in. The entrance holes were hidden, but if the sett was busy there would have been spoil heaps of freshly dug earth lolling down the slope and shaped like the panting tongues of big dogs. There were none.

An old wall and a line of beech trees, one of them huge, defined the clearing's western edge. I was fifty yards from the nearest beech, a hundred and fifty from the rowan in the clearing. I was intent on the rowan and its immediate surroundings when I felt an awareness, as tangible as an itch, one of the fruits of hundreds of badger-watching hours. It is the most priceless of the tools of the nature-writing trade, that nudge in the ribs, that tap on the shoulder, that impulse to stop what you're doing and change direction because you are looking in the wrong place. So I looked along the line of the wall, and there at the base of the third beech trunk was the head, chest and forepaws of a substantial badger, sitting upright and staring at me.

In this kind of situation, my job becomes almost laughably easy, for it demands of me that I do nothing at all, other than watch and remember. The badger has the difficult job, which is to assess the threat I pose (if any), and what to make of my shape's intrusion in his landscape. Perhaps he (I was convinced at once he was a big boar) had just caught sight of me at that moment as he peered round the beech tree. Or he may have seen my slow-paced and quiet arrival and my subsequent stillness. Critically, the east wind did not bring him my scent but rather blew it away from him, and my stillness made no sound. He looked relaxed. He sat back like a bear and scratched under his chin and in his chest fur. He stood, shook himself like a wet dog, then resumed his original position.

His eyes had never left me, but badger eyes only tell a badger so much.

He advanced a few paces out into the open so that I should be in no doubt about his size and his power, so that I would recognise his overlordship of this neck of the woods. He raised his muzzle and sniffed the air painstakingly. But if it told him anything at all other than "hyacinth" I would be very surprised. His choice was to go back underground and lie low for a bit if I troubled him enough, or circle furtively behind me for a clearer scent, but he would know too that in the woods behind me every other scent was overpowered by the flowers. So he did neither. He decided I was no threat, turned in his own length, and trudged away so that at once he was hidden by wall and trees. I waited to see if he would reappear, crossing the clearing, but he did not. So I followed a hunch.

I crossed the slope above the wall with all the discretion I could muster until I could see the area where he had been. I was delighted to find that he was still there, still grooming himself, that he had only moved a few yards, and that he was sitting in the midst of what was clearly a very well populated badger village. There were holes everywhere, heaps and heaps of fresh earth, many of the heaps grooved and flattened by the high jinks of cubs. The centre of activity was on his side of the wall, but there were three more outlying entrances on my side, and each one had its own welcome mat of excavated earth.

So the badger survey had got it wrong.

It wasn't that the sett had gone cold, it was just that it had moved. And it had moved no more than a hundred yards uphill and, demonstrably, it was thriving. I watched for another hour. The boar did wander off eventually, but straight into the woods. My initial thought had been that he was the first to emerge, for I had arrived there early. But after a subsequent badgerless hour, it looked as if he might have been the last, or at least the last to leave the area of the sett. But I didn't care. I had found what I came for. It was enough to know that all was well, and to know that in an east wind there was a fine seat on a fallen tree trunk where I could watch whenever I chose.

I went back the following day in the middle of the afternoon, hours before the badgers would surface, and explored the old sett. Most of the holes I remembered were overgrown, but two I didn't remember were obviously in use. There was also a dead-straight beaten path directly from the old core of the sett to the new sett under the big beech. How could anyone surveying badgers miss that? Unless, of course, the old sett had indeed been abandoned utterly for a few weeks or a few months, and the beaten path was a new one laid down by a new group of badgers exploring outwards from the sett under the beech. Perhaps those two new holes in the old sett were nursery holes, perhaps they were where a couple of the older badgers in the group had moved, or perhaps the new sett was already so populous that it was necessary to build an extension.

As an old friend who lives nearby once told me, by way of explaining why some setts are left cold for years and then suddenly they are rediscovered:

"Once a badger sett, always a badger sett."

BADGER

I'll come back one day when the midges have gone, the bracken is flat, the barn owls are moping along the woodland edge and the midwinter badger sett has a comatose air.

AFTERWORD

THE BADGER (*Meles meles*) is a mustelid, a member of the weasel family, a diverse tribe ranging in size from weasels and stoats to pine martens, otters and wolverines.

It is widely distributed across Europe and Asia. In Britain it is remarkably common considering how few people actually see one. It is primarily nocturnal, but in spring and summer it is often out and about before sunset.

The badger is a sociable beast in that it lives colonially in underground setts, but it is a solitary beast in that it travels alone, hunts and feeds alone, and sometimes lives alone.

It is a true omnivore with the incisors and canines of a carnivore and the flattened molars of a herbivore. Food ranges from earthworms and slugs to cereal, fruit, vegetation and nuts, to carrion and small birds and mammals that are either too slow or too sick to escape its often indiscreet approach. The badger is also a pacifist, but pound for pound, there are few stronger mammals in the wildwood, and it is a foolish creature that picks a fight with one, because although its first reaction is to turn the other cheek or entreat for peace, when it decides to fight, its inner warrior surfaces, and it doesn't lose many battles.

Humanity's relationship with the badger is essentially one of extremes. On one hand it is legally protected, and organisations like the Badger Trust and Scottish Badgers are dedicated to their wellbeing. On the other, there are what an ex-policeman I used to know would refer to as "the terrier boys" – badger baiters who gather at setts with their dogs and the objective of tormenting badgers to death. David Stephen once told me that, "the man who deliberately sends a terrier to ground to face a badger should resign from the human race." He got no argument from me.

Then there is bovine tuberculosis in the south-west of England. In farcical pursuit of reducing its incidence to a more manageable level, the

BADGER

British Government authorised a rolling cull of badgers in 2013, on the basis that they acted as carriers of the disease. Neither the government nor the farming industry in that part of the world comes out of this with much credit. Bovine TB is a disease of cattle, not of badgers, and a more considered approach to farming techniques is the only thing that will ultimately achieve any measure of control. The cull has been a public relations disaster for all concerned, and solved nothing.

But then there are the good guys. Back in 1908, the then Secretary of the Bank of England wrote a book that (among many other achievements) changed the way much of the country thought about badgers. His name was Kenneth Grahame and his book was *The Wind in the Willows*. The book was a slow starter until it was very publicly endorsed by two very significant men from remarkably different backgrounds. One was A.A. Milne, the author of *Winnie the Pooh,* and the other was the President of the United States, Theodore Roosevelt. The book has since travelled the world,

57

and its endearing portrait of Mr Badger includes this snatch of philosophy addressed to the Mole:

There's no security, or peace and tranquillity, except underground… No builders, no tradesmen, no remarks passed on you by fellows looking over your wall, and above all, no weather.

There was also this advice to the Mole from the Water Rat as he tried to curb the Mole's determination to meet Mr Badger:

Badger'll turn up some day or other – he's always turning up… But you must not only take him as *you find him, but* when *you find him.*

When I began to write a badger book of my own (*Badgers on the Highland Edge*, Jonathan Cape, 1994), I was bombarded by advice from badger-watchers of all hues who suddenly emerged from the woodwork, but none of it was more sage and of more to use to me than the Water Rat's to the Mole.

BADGER

If the architects of the government's badger cull had ever taken the trouble to read *The Wind in the Willows* – or better still, if they should take the trouble to read it now – they would find food for thought about the folly and futility of their actions in the following passage, in which the Badger offers sage words to the Mole about the ways of the people.

"*Very long ago, on the spot where the Wild Wood waves now, before ever it had planted itself and grown up to what it now is, there was a city – a city of people, you know. Here, where we are standing, they lived, and walked, and talked, and slept, and carried on their business. Here they stabled their horses and feasted, from here they rode out to fight or drove out to trade. They were a powerful people, and rich, and great builders. They built to last, for they thought their city would last forever.*"

"*But what has become of them all?*" asked the Mole.

"*Who can tell?*" said the Badger. "*People come – they stay for a while, they flourish, they build – and then they go. It is their way. But we remain. There were badgers here, I've been told, long before that same city ever came to be. And now there are badgers here again. We are an enduring lot, and we may move out for a time, but we wait, and are patient, and back we come. And so it will ever be."*

No one who becomes fascinated by badgers gets very far without encountering the work of Ernest Neal. His book, *Badgers* (Blandford Press, 1977), was an instant classic, and although it has since been updated as *The Natural History of Badgers*, the original set a meticulously observed and persuasive example of what a naturalist's monograph should be.

Early in 1995 I received a letter that began:

I was given your badger book at Christmas. I just wanted to thank you for saying kind things about me and to say how much I enjoyed reading it.

It took me right back to those early days – 1936 onwards – when any time I watched the badgers it was an adventure and a chance to add a tiny detail to the badger jigsaw about which so little was known then. Your studies were so refreshingly personal – a quest which rang a bell with me even after fifty-plus years of watching badgers...

BADGER

It was signed *Ernest G. Neal.*

The letter is beside me as I write this. It lives inside the front cover of my only copy of my own book. He was the world authority on the subject, and I knew next to nothing (my badger book was about finding out about badgers), but his letter made me a lifelong disciple of the badger's cause, and I suspect he knew it might. And now, twenty-one years after he wrote it, here I am putting another few pieces of the jigsaw puzzle together into another book about badgers, so I guess you could say that it worked.

JIM CRUMLEY IS A NATURE WRITER, journalist, poet, and passionate advocate for our wildlife and wild places. He is the author of more than thirty books, and is a newspaper and magazine columnist and an occasional broadcaster on both BBC radio and television.

He has written companions to this volume on the barn owl, fox, hare, swan and skylark, and there are further ENCOUNTERS IN THE WILD titles planned. He has also written in depth on topics as diverse as beavers, eagles, wolves, whales, native woods, mountains and species reintroductions, as well as *The Nature of Autumn*.

Published by Saraband
Suite 202, 98 Woodlands Road
Glasgow, G3 6HB
www.saraband.net

ISBN: 9781910192627

Printed in the EU on sustainably sourced paper.
Cover illustration: © Carry Akroyd